Around the World in Poems

A Selection for Young Children

Illustrations by Joelle Crahay

A Note on Translations

Many of the poems in this book were originally written in languages other than English. They have been translated with care and respect for the original works, with the aim of preserving their spirit, imagery, and beauty while making them accessible and enjoyable for young readers.

Some poems come from oral traditions passed down through generations. In these cases, the original author and language may be unknown. The translations presented here reflect the best available sources and interpretations and may not always match the original word for word, but seek to honor the meaning and feeling of the poems.

Illustrations by Joelle Crahay

About this book

I began searching for a poetry book to read to my grandchildren, something gentle, timeless, and filled with poems from many places. While there are countless beautiful poetry collections for children, I longed for one that gathered voices from around the world, alongside poems echoing the charm of earlier generations. My father was a poet. I didn't inherit his writing talent, but I do share his love of poetry. I still remember, with great fondness, the verses of my own childhood.

Growing up in Belgium, I cherished the poems of Jacques Prévert, Jules Renard, and many others. That nostalgia inspired me to gather a small collection of poetic "little gems" from different cultures and eras.

Some of the poems in this book have accompanied me since I was young; others I discovered along the way and wanted to share, to give them a new life in the hands of children. For the illustrations, I chose to reflect my own personal style. My book includes watercolor paintings, simple drawings, and paper collages, some more forgiving than others! None are perfect, but all were created with joy and reflect my own evolving artistic journey. I hope this book brings delight, wonder, and a love of poetry to the children in your life.

The Zebra

The zebra runs free,
His stripes gleam bright.
He dances the plain
From day to night.

African Folk Verse
(oral tradition, 19th-century collection)

The Lion

The lion is strong,
The lion is bold.
He guards the plain,
His mane is gold.

African Folk Verse
(oral tradition, 19th-century collection)

The Giraffe

The giraffe walks tall,
Her neck to the sky.
She sees the horizon,
The clouds passing by.

African Folk Verse
(oral tradition, 19th-century collection)

The Crocodile

The crocodile swims,
With eyes open wide.
He waits in the river,
Half in and half hide.

African Folk Verse
(oral tradition, 19th-century collection)

Rainy Season Love Song

The rain is in love with you, darling,
It's kissing you everywhere—
Rain pattering on your small brown feet,
Rain dancing in your curly hair.

Gladys Casely-Hayford (Sierra Leone, 1904-1950)

Winter Song

Rain and wind, and wind and rain.
Will the Summer come again?
Rain on houses, on the street,
Wetting all the people's feet,
Though they run with might and main.
Rain and wind, and wind and rain.

Katherine Mansfield (New Zealand, 1888-1923) — excerpt

The Song of the Bee

Buzz! buzz! buzz!
This is the song of the bee.
His legs are of yellow,
A jolly good fellow,
And yet a great worker is he.
Buzz! buzz! buzz!
From morning's first light until late,
He works every minute,
There's honey all in it,
And plenty for you on your plate.
Buzz! buzz! buzz!
The bumblebee sings in the clover.
Though summer be past,
He keeps singing to last,
Till the warm sunny days are all over.
Buzz! buzz! buzz!
He hums and he never complains.
With a spirit so fine,
He makes clover divine,
And honey to sweeten our pains.

Marian Douglas, pen name of Annie Douglas Green Robinson (United States, 1842-1913) — excerpt

The Sparrow

A tiny bird upon the eave,
Hides beneath the thatch to weave,
A nest so small, so snug, so round,
Where chirps of joy and life resound.
It hops about from twig to grain,
And sings again when rain is done.

Jovan Jovanović Zmaj (Serbia, 1833-1904)

The Frog

The old pond—
A frog jumps in,
Sound of water.

Matsuo Bashō (Japan, 1644-1694)— excerpt

Pussy has a whiskered face

Pussy has a whiskered face,
And Pussy has four feet;
To walk withal on the soft sand,
And leave no mark nor trace
When she goes o'er
the grass or the wheat,
Or the garden flowers neat.

Christina Rossetti (England, 1830-1894)

If a Pig Wore a Wig

If a pig wore a wig,
what could we say?
Treat him as a gentleman,
and say "Good day."
If his tail chanced to fail,
What could we do? —
Send him to the tailoress
To get one new.

Christina Rossetti (England, 1830-1894)

The Butterfly's Wedding

We're going to marry you today,
Little butterfly bright and gay;
We're going to marry you, it's true—
Your bridesmaids will be flowers too.

Amado Nervo (Mexico, 1870-1919) — excerpt

The Butterfly

A love letter,
folded tight,
finds a flower
in morning light.

Jules Renard (France, 1864-1910)

The Damselfly

Blue needle,
slim and still,
resting by the pond at will.
The air hums low,
the water gleams,
she hovers lightly
in her dreams.

Jules Renard (France, 1864-1910)

The Glow-worm

Look! It's already night,
yet his little house has light.
A drop of moon has fallen
into the grass!

Jules Renard (France, 1864-1910)

Two Little Clouds

Two little clouds one summer's day,
Went flying through the sky;
They went so fast they bumped their heads,
And both began to cry.

Old Father Sun looked out and said:
"Oh! never mind, my dears,
I'll send my little fairy folk
To dry your falling tears."

Elizabeth M. Hadley (USA, circa early 20th century) — excerpt

The Little Golden Bird

Wake me up very early—
I want to go out to the field,
To see that golden little bird
That sings at morning's first reveal.
They say there's nothing half so bright,
No sweeter song at dawn's first light...

Rafael Pombo (Colombia, 1833-1912) — excerpt

The Rainbow

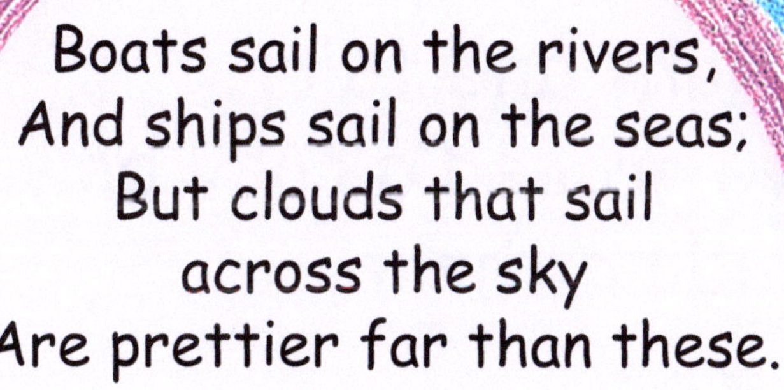

Boats sail on the rivers,
And ships sail on the seas;
But clouds that sail
across the sky
Are prettier far than these.

Christina Rossetti (England, 1830-1894) — excerpt

The Wind

Who has seen the wind?
Neither you nor I;
but when the trees
bow down their heads,
the wind is passing by.

Christina Rossetti (England, 1830-1894) — excerpt

The Violet

Down in a green and shady bed
A modest violet grew;
Its stalk was bent, it hung its head
As if to hide from view.
And yet it was a lovely flower,
Its colors bright and fair;
It might have graced a rosy bower,
Instead of hiding there.

Jane Taylor (England, 1783-1824)

Violets
And the violets themselves,
Blooming like magic.
In the grass overnight,
Do you see them?
You bend down,
And like me you wonder:
Are they not, this spring,
A brighter blue?

Sidonie-Gabrielle Colette (France, 1873-1954)
excerpt — layout adaptation

The Kite

And up into the blue sky
each child sends up his kite.
See it sway and dip and jump,
rising again to meet the wind...

Giovanni Pascoli (Italy, 1855-1912)
excerpt from L'aquilone

The Swing

How do you like to go up in a swing,
Up in the air so blue?
Oh, I do think it the pleasantest thing
Ever a child can do!
Up in the air and over the wall,
Till I can see so wide,
Rivers and trees and cattle and all
Over the countryside—
Till I look down on the garden green,
Down on the roof so brown—
Up in the air I go flying again,
Up in the air and down!

Robert Louis Stevenson (Scotland, 1850–1894)

Spring

There is waving of grass in the breeze
And a song in the air,
And a murmur of myriad bees
That toil everywhere.

Banjo Paterson (Australia, 1864-1941) — excerpt

Very Early Spring

The hedges are all whispering,
the twigs begin to sing;
a silver note of something new—
the very first of spring.

Katherine Mansfield (New Zealand, 1888-1923) — excerpt

The Little Turtle

There was a little turtle,
He lived in a box.
He swam in the puddles
And climbed on the rocks.

He snapped at a mosquito,
He snapped at a flea,
He snapped at a minnow,
And he snapped at me.

He caught the mosquito,
He caught the flea,
He caught the minnow—
But he didn't catch me!

Vachel Lindsay (USA, 1879-1931)

The Potatoes' Dance

Potatoes were the waiters,
Potatoes were the band,
Potatoes were the dancers
Kicking up the sand.
Their legs were old burnt matches,
Their arms were just the same.
They jigged and whirled and scrambled
In honor of the dame,
The noble Irish lady,
The laughing Irish lady
Who makes potatoes prance.

Cherry Blossoms

A cloud of blossoms —
is that the distant mist,
or spring in the air?

Matsuo Bashō (Japan, 1644-1694)

Spring Morning

This spring morning I woke in bed,
to birdsong ringing overhead.
After wind and rain through night so wild,
how many blossoms lost, O gentle child?

Meng Haoran (China, 689-740, Tang dynasty)

My Mother

Who ran to help me when I fell,
And would some pretty story tell,
Or kiss the place to make it well?—
My mother.

Who taught my infant lips to pray,
And love God's holy book and day,
And walk in wisdom's pleasant way?—
My mother.

Ann Taylor (England, 1782-1866) — excerpt

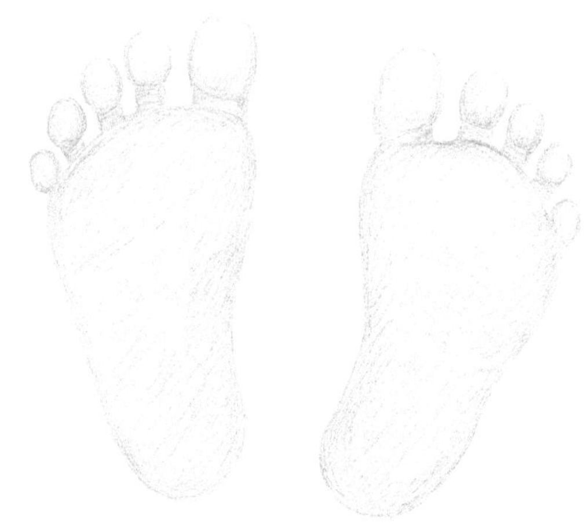

Baby and Mamma

What a little thing am I!
Hardly higher than the table;
I can eat, and play, and cry,
But to work I am not able.
Nothing in the world I know,
But mamma will try and show me.
Sweet mamma, I love her so,
She's so very kind unto me.
And she sets me on her knee,
Very often, for some kisses.
Oh! how good I'll try to be,
For such a dear mamma as this is.

Jane Taylor (England, 1783-1824) — excerpt

The Song Fairy

There was a fairy, bright and free,
With tangled weeds upon her head;
She ran through bushes merrily,
So no one caught her as she fled.
In April's time, she came to teach
The birds their songs in field and beech.

And when the birds all bravely tried,
But sang a note that wandered wrong,
The fairy scolded them (and sighed),
"Not so! Not so!" — and fixed their song.
She fussed and taught with patient cheer
Those naughty pupils, far and near.

Armand Silvestre (France, 1837-1901) — excerpt
rhyming English translation

Mary's Lamb

Mary had a little lamb,
Its fleece was white as snow,
And everywhere that Mary went
The lamb was sure to go;
He followed her to school one day—
That was against the rule,
It made the children laugh and play,
To see a lamb at school.

Sarah Josepha Hale (USA, 1788-1879) — excerpt

Cradle Song

Sleep, sleep, little one,
The sky is dark above you.
The walrus hunts, the seal dives deep,
But here is rest and safety.
Sleep, sleep, little one.

Inuit Traditional (collected by Knud Rasmussen, early 20th century)

Sleep, Little One

Sleep, little one, sleep,
while the stars their vigil keep.
Dream of forests, dream of streams,
wrapped in nature's tender dreams.

The Moon

The moon is round, the moon is bright,
She shines upon the earth at night.
She watches children in their beds,
And guards the dreams above their heads.

Both poems above are Ojibwe Traditional (19th-century collection)

My Evening

I

The day was full of lightning bright,
now stars peep out into the night,
the quiet stars that softly gleam.
The frogs croak low, half-lost in dream.

II

The poplar leaves begin to sway,
a gentle joy drifts through the day.
The little houses softly glow —
evening whispers, slow and low.

Giovanni Pascoli (Italy, 1855-1912) — excerpt from La mia sera (1900)

Song of the Stars

Stars above in chorus sing,
Voices bright on silver wing.
Guiding children through the night,
Till the morning brings them light.

Aboriginal Traditional (Australia, 19th-century collection)

Bedtime

I really don't want to go to bed,
I'm still playing with Teddy instead!
Why should I put my toys away,
when tomorrow is another play day?
My book is great—Pirates, beware!
I'll swish and whoosh with heroic flair!
But now my blanket feels warm and deep,
and Teddy is yawning... time for sleep.
So on my pillow I rest my head,
all snug and safe in my little bed.
I'll dream of ships and oceans wide—
with Captain Teddy by my side.

Joelle Crahay (USA, contemporary)

The Star

Twinkle, twinkle, little star,
How I wonder what you are!
Up above the world so high,
Like a diamond in the sky.
When the blazing sun is gone,
When he nothing shines upon,
Then you show your little light,
Twinkle, twinkle, all the night.
Then the traveler in the dark
Thanks you for your tiny spark;
He could not see which way to go,
If you did not twinkle so.
In the dark blue sky you keep,
And often through my curtains peep,
For you never shut your eye
Till the sun is in the sky.
As your bright and tiny spark
Lights the traveler in the dark,
Though I know not what you are,
Twinkle, twinkle, little star.

Jane Taylor (England, 1783-1824)

Bed in Summer

In winter I get up at night,
And dress by yellow candle-light.
In summer quite the other way,
I have to go to bed by day.
I have to go to bed and see
The birds still hopping on the tree,
Or hear the grown-up people's feet
Still going past me in the street.
And does it not seem hard to you,
When all the sky is clear and blue,
And I should like so much to play,
To have to go to bed by day?

Robert Louis Stevenson (Scotland, 1850–1894)

Canoe Song

The sea is wide, the sea is deep,
The waves will rock us all to sleep.
The gulls are calling, bright and free,
They guide our boat across the sea.

Yámana Traditional (Patagonia, oral tradition)

About the poets

Matsuo Bashō (Japan, 1644–1694)
A master of haiku whose delicate poems reflect nature, simplicity, and calm reflection.

Gladys Casely-Hayford (Ghana–Sierra Leone, 1904–1950)
A poet who celebrated African identity with warmth, rhythm, and cultural pride.

Sidonie-Gabrielle Colette (France, 1873–1954)
A French writer known for vivid, sensory language and sharp observations of nature and life.

Marian Douglas (United States, 1842–1913)
An American poet who wrote gentle, musical verse for children, often inspired by nature and the small wonders of everyday life.

Sarah Josepha Hale (United States, 1788–1879)
An American writer and editor best known for children's verse, including "Mary Had a Little Lamb."

Elizabeth M. Hadley (United States, early 20th century)
An American poet whose light, playful lines were written for young readers.

Archibald Lampman (Canada, 1861–1899)
A Canadian poet celebrated for serene, contemplative verses about landscapes and seasons.

Vachel Lindsay (United States, 1879–1931)
An American poet who brought rhythm, music, and playful energy into his poems.

Katherine Mansfield (New Zealand, 1888–1923)
A modernist writer whose delicate words capture fleeting emotions and hidden beauty.

Meng Haoran (China, 689–740)
A Tang-dynasty poet known for peaceful verses inspired by mountains, rivers, and quiet mornings.

Amado Nervo (Mexico, 1870–1919)
A Mexican poet whose gentle, lyrical verses often explore love, nature, and the inner world, blending imagination with quiet emotion.

Giovanni Pascoli (Italy, 1855–1912)
An Italian poet who wrote about childhood memories, country life, and the soft voice of nature.

Banjo Paterson (Australia, 1864–1941)
An Australian poet famous for vivid, memorable verse that brings the outdoors to life.

Rafael Pombo (Colombia, 1833–1912)
A beloved Colombian poet known for charming poems for children and fables in verse.

Jules Renard (France, 1864–1910)
A French writer whose vivid, delicate observations turn everyday scenes into
small literary jewels.

Christina Rossetti (England, 1830–1894)
A beloved English poet known for lyrical, tender verses filled with imagery and emotion.

Armand Silvestre (France, 1837–1901)
A French poet and writer known for light, musical verse.

Robert Louis Stevenson (Scotland, 1850–1894)
Known for adventure tales and joyful poems about childhood, nature, and imagination.

Ann Taylor (England, 1782–1866)
An English poet who wrote tender, moral, and charming verses for children.

Jane Taylor (England, 1783–1824)
Best known for "Twinkle, Twinkle, Little Star," she wrote simple, musical poems
adored by generations.

Jovan Jovanović Zmaj (Serbia, 1833–1904)
A beloved Serbian poet known for joyful, musical poems for children.

Traditional Poetry

Aboriginal Tradition (Australia)
Poems rooted in the deep connection between Australia's First Peoples and the land, sky, and ancestral spirit.

African Folk Verse (Africa)
Poetry passed down through generations, carrying stories, rhythm, and wisdom from diverse African cultures.

Inuit Traditional Poetry (Arctic regions)
Verses shaped by ice, sea, wind, and the stories Inuit families have shared for countless generations.

Ojibwe Tradition (North America)
Poems celebrating nature, animals, and the spirit that connects all living things.

Yámana Tradition (Tierra del Fuego)
Traditional verses inspired by the sea, islands, and ancestral memory of the Yamana people.

Thank you for choosing this book!

I hope it brings joy, curiosity, and a love of poetry into your home.
If you enjoyed it, please consider leaving a review; your feedback means so much.

We also write and illustrate the Teddy the Tortoise picture-book series:

- Book 1: Teddy the Tortoise — Misadventure on Amelia Island
- Book 2: Teddy Meets Mitzy — Adventure on Amelia Island
- Book 3: Teddy's Birthday — Party Time on Amelia Island
- Book 4: Teddy and Marcus — Racing Time on Amelia Island
- Book 5: Count and Share with Teddy — An Interactive Number Book
  (written by Janet Weinstein • illustrated by Joelle and Andrew Weinstein)
- Book 6: Teddy's Tummy Troubles — Caring Time on Amelia Island (Coming 2026)
- Book 7: Teddy's Nighttime Stroll — Moonlight Magic on Amelia Island
  (Coming 2026)
- Teddy and Friends Coloring Book

For more information, please visit:
TalesofAmeliaIsland.com